PLANET AUSCHWITZ

poems by

Gary Myers

Finishing Line Press
Georgetown, Kentucky

PLANET AUSCHWITZ

Copyright © 2022 by Gary Myers
ISBN 979-8-88838-017-8 First Edition
All rights reserved under International and Pan-American Copyright Conventions. No part of this book may be reproduced in any manner whatsoever without written permission from the publisher, except in the case of brief quotations embodied in critical articles and reviews.

ACKNOWLEDGMENTS

California Quarterly "Selection"
Illya's Honey Quarterly "The Portrait" and "Prisoner 44070"

Publisher: Leah Huete de Maines
Editor: Christen Kincaid
Cover Art: Tim Myers
Author Photo: Jackie Croxdale
Cover Design: Tim Myers

Order online: www.finishinglinepress.com
also available on amazon.com

Author inquiries and mail orders:
Finishing Line Press
P. O. Box 1626
Georgetown, Kentucky 40324
U. S. A.

Table of Contents

View of the Planet 1

Windows 2

Shooting Stars 3

Hair 4

The Leaf 5

Crossing the Vistula 6

Castanets 7

Quixote 8

Mr. Philips Radio 9

Postcards 10

Prisoner 44070 11

Collectibles 12

Black Flower 13

Canada 14

Selection 15

Little Wood 16

Clouds 17

Distant Music 18

The Bademeister 19

Clay Faces 20

Roma 21

Dr. Injection 22

The Secret 23

Her Face 24

Planet Auschwitz 25

Angels 26

Anne Frank 27

The Stairs of Death 28

Mittweida	29
Touched	30
Awake in Lebensborn	31
The White Rose	32
The Way Back	33
The Portrait	34
Blondi	35
Franziska Braun	36
White Rooms	37
The Pond	38
Blackbirds	39
Spectacles	40
Artifact	41
Whiteout	42
Schindler's Grave	43
The Blue Room	44
A.K.A. Ricardo Klement	45
Hairball	46
Woman in a Red Coat	47
Questions	48
Majdanek's Ghosts	49
The Answer	50

In Memory of Howard Moss

"If you wish to find the spark in our life, look in the ashes."
—Fred Englard
*Survivor of the Lodz Ghetto and
Auschwitz and Siegmar-Schoenau Concentration Camps*

View of the Planet

"We have before us an ordeal of the most grievous kind. We have before us many, many long months of struggle and of suffering."
   —Winston Churchill

Seen from space a cloud mass
Slowly turns above the Atlantic
Like the smoke trail of something large
Screwed into the surface of the planet

Further east   greater Europe
Veiled in layers of mist
Glimpsed now and then
In mottled shades of green

Faces a dark time
The expanding edge of night
That approaches with no sound
Engulfing half of the planet

That rotates slowly
Under a watchful eye
And somewhere   below the clouds
A man pounds the podium

Shouts his promise of domination
To thousands of followers   cheering
Their hands raised high in salute
For what's come over them

Windows

Families in Polish ghettos avoided arrest by Nazi SS by covering light sources and isolating themselves in various rooms of their houses.

Outside a dark atmosphere
Its ashen fingers of smoke
Feel their way along the ground
And rise curiously before windows

Cracked from bomb blasts
And smudged by children's faces
Who draw near for a closer look
They want to examine the night

Beyond their isolation and silence
Their curiosity pulls them closer
In rooms hung with thick curtains
And dimmed by shrouded lamps

But a gap in the curtains could mean
A moment's betrayal   a glint of light
Appearing to the watchful
Like a distant star whose light is

Seen obliquely by a trick of the eye
And tied to the distance noticed
Suddenly through the smoke
As one child's spark of courage

Shooting Stars

> All Jews, and other "undesirables," were made to wear color-coded stars in order to identify their alleged offense and, later, condemn them to the concentration camps.

Some say a star guides one through life
On a summer night you have your choice
However distant   and the luck it brings
Brings happiness   unless pinned to your lapel

A yellow hexagram stamped "Jude"
Marking the man on a ghetto street
And the woman in the market   child on hip
For a fate unknown to them and others

Even the children are tagged
And run from street to alley
Playing wildly through the dusty
Atmosphere of a familiar despair

Then one meets the corpus of this galaxy
Moving en masse toward the train yard
Each with world in tow   in bags or on carts
Each family its own constellation

Their fate resolved on Nazi star charts
Posted in the Chancellery office   the colored stars
Determining the destiny of each
At Buchenwald Ravensbrück and beyond

Hair

> *During camp liberations several tons of hair cut from the heads of prisoners were found.*

One girl's hair   braided by careful hands
And tied with a white ribbon at the small of her back
Swings in rhythm as she strolls
A Berlin boulevard on a spring morning

At times her braid falls forward into view
As when she studies some red flowers
Spilling from a black window box
Their color dazzling enough to turn anyone's head

And her hair   traced by its own glow
As rich an auburn as anyone could dream
She impulsively strokes   feeling the braid
Down the long rope of its beauty

One flower she considers carefully
Leaning forward to inspect its petals
While pulling her long braid taut with both hands
Another she daubs with its brush-end

Before tossing the braid over her shoulder
And gliding past the Brown Shirts
Patrolling the district that morning
One gesturing with fingers like scissors

The Leaf

> *In the Warsaw ghetto very little grew, and the children craved seeing flowers, grass–anything with color. One girl attempted to retrieve a leaf for her dying sister.*

The idea of a leaf bringing happiness
And its shade of green delighting
A child who lay dying in her ghetto bed
Sent one sister under a wall to the Aryan side

Carefully removing loose bricks she scooted through
Destined for the park where trees stood
Basking in the low hum of summer
There she would find the perfect leaf for her sister

The greenest to flicker in the wind somehow
Catching her eye at the end of a branch
Where its delicate shape and slight curve
Would invite her to look carefully   even touch it

The way she touched the waxy face of her dying sister
That leaf would fall into her opened hand
And lie there for her to carry home   to the other side
Where she would place it in a glass beside her sister's bed

So she entered the park to the sounds
Of laughter   children playing
Under a canopy of leaves plentiful enough
To arrest even the powers that be

Crossing the Vistula

In 1940 a continuous flow of Jews into the ghettos for resettlement was a common sight.

So many horse-drawn wagons
One wonders whether
Nomads from a past century
Or the remnants of families

Exiled to Krakow's ghetto where
Behind shrouded windows and brick walls
The fading glow of life and God's will
Escapes the inspired

Like smoke up the chimney
Clearly the light touch of the whip
Across a horse crossing the Vistula
Makes all appear from a different time

The surface of the river
Sliding by like a sheet of metal
Glinting facets of light under clouds
Rock-heavy in color and threatening

How many arrive each day
Is multiplied by generations
An endless caravan through time
Of those who would become us all

Castanets

Facing arrest and death by the Gestapo, children in the ghettos
entertained themselves by making toys.

Two pieces of hardwood stolen from the Wood Works
One between the forefinger and middle finger
The other held loosely with middle and ring finger
Then a quick twist of the hand to send clicking

Through the cavernous streets of the Lodz ghetto
As though percussive sounds were an observance
Among children aware of imminent doom   an intuited
Recognition of the darkness permeating each brick

Each room behind each window and deeper into the spaces
That hang as huge voids within families
Drawing the very energy of happiness into one dominant
And growing absence they know will be theirs

Today   tomorrow   or during the night
When the sound of boots in the street
Ricochet off the window panes
Or the gloved hand of a passerby tests the door latch

With a quick twist   disturbing the morning silence
Each day the children wheel their toys in the faces of strangers
The manic clatter of castanets rising into the dull air
Each day vigilant against the inevitable

Quixote

> *Odd assortments of personal effects were collected upon arrival at the camps. At Auschwitz one suitcase contained a copy of Don Quixote.*

Not all dreams ride the back of prose
Or gallop in haste away from reality
Though transport to unknown places
Might make one choose Cervantes

A moment's decision   if one has room
For one book among personal effects
Packed neatly into a small suitcase
Allowed only what one can carry

The decisions appear as arbitrary
As expected   a photo album   a locket
A simple flat-knit sweater and gloves
Seen one last time in perfect arrangement

Before closing the lid and walking with others
To the station that hangs in the mist
Like some ghostly inn posting vacancies
For countless guests   who keep arriving

Under armed guard and the burden
Of their belongings gathered quickly
Not with illusions of nobility or adventure
But in the service of the heart

Mr. Philips Radio

> *Jan Zwartendijk forged over 2,400 "Curaçao visas" for Jews escaping Lithuania. His code name recalls one "Righteous Among the Nations" for helping so many Jews.*

What the anonymous know they are not telling
If only to fade a little further from view
Or have the sound of their voices finally forgotten
The anonymous know not to speak

But they are there   turning the corner
For home   hurrying up a distant hill
Each unknown with new papers
A Curaçao visa for safe passage abroad

Each one the creation of Mr. Philips Radio
Whose persona blurs in a smokey cafe
Grows inaudible amid the jingle of flatware
Each one the subject of his plan

As they lower their voices
Hide their faces   and disappear
Within the chiaroscuro of afternoon and later
When newspaper headlines of Nazi takeover

Stand like flimsy buildings in their laps
They await their rendezvous   hardly noticed
If one could only hear their voices
If one only knew who they'd become

Postcards

> *The Nazis sent forged postcards to families whose friends and relatives were deported to camps. They were always positive about "resettlement."*

One might expect nothing more of friends
Departing Warsaw on a crowded train
Than a fond farewell for the journey
In promise of work and resettlement

One might even regret staying behind
When later a postcard arrives
Recounting a long yet pleasant passage
Though scrawled by an unfamiliar hand

The words of happiness too brief
To escape suspicion
Too cold in their account of the weather
Not to show indifference

Unlike an earlier time
Lost in the wash of years   when friends
Together on a ghetto street were buoyed
By a bright sun and an azure sky

Pristine as a dome of glass
Forever balanced between heaven and earth
When there was no concern walking beneath it
Or its fragile tempera ever cracking

Prisoner 44070

For Edith Stein who was raised a Jew and studied philosophy before becoming a Carmelite nun and a victim of the Holocaust at Auschwitz. She was canonized a Saint by Pope John Paul II on October 11, 1998.

Perhaps the silence of the dead reminds the heart
To listen carefully   to know each absence
As one's own while alone in the world
Drawn between the present and the hereafter

Perhaps the answer to philosophy's question fades
And finally wilts   like a rose   or Rosa your sister
When arrested and sent with you to Westerbork
Perhaps survival defies every explanation

But one reason somehow transcends all others
To float in the ether of a new desire for God
A desire that expands the mind's image of death
Beyond the cruelties at Terezin and Auschwitz

Perhaps your truth came as a last resort
Tending to children in the train car
Your hands aglow with the dim light
Through a roof hatch   the moon's powder

Dusting the head of a child in your lap   his face
Floating in the darkness   a luminous pool of sorrow
Around which all others gather and find
Within your calming shade their own reflections

Collectibles

> *All those transported to camps were stripped of their belongings and, though promised their return, they were sorted by category for shipment to Berlin.*

First the small personal items like watches and rings
Then such possessions as forks and knives
Needed for resettlement in the east
Such things one can recover later   upon arrival

What luggage one brings must be examined
At rail stops during the long journey
To Ravensbrück   Buchenwald   Auschwitz
And claimed during final inspection

New accommodations and possessions
Will be provided those who need them
Who keep moving from one staging area to the next
Next the coats must come off   especially those made of fur

Expensive as they were   they are too warm for the train
Sweaters are even discouraged
Upon arrival one's clothes will be collected for disinfection
One's glasses and shoes for repair and cleaning

One's hair   for protection against vermin
And after selection and the business at hand
Everything else collected and sorted
Gathered into boxes for safe keeping

Black Flower

> *The search light in the Birkenau gatehouse, so-called because its heat louvers gave it a bristled appearance, greeted incoming trains.*

How dark the apprehension of a single light
Scanning the Polish countryside
A fiery spotlight atop the Birkenau gatehouse
Marking the train east of the entrance

Like the light from a door left ajar
Inviting everyone through a night whose gloom
Is the very substance of their destination
How unexpected the black flower's appearance

Searching the fields to the right and left as one passes
Beneath the looming tower of the gatehouse
Each secret on the horizon momentarily arrested within
A column of light that falls silently into the distance

Sweeping all into the scrutiny of its glare
Even the name searchlight suggests a need
An emptiness that flashes across a landscape
With the consuming suddenness of death

How numbing to see heat rising from its louvers
Rippling the winter air around the guards
Who direct its stark light into a world
Ever dark and defenseless

Canada

Upon arrival at Auschwitz, prisoners' valuables were sorted and stored in a separate complex called Canada before shipment back to Germany.

So-called the Land of Plenty
Prisoners sorted mounds of belongings
Collected with each train's arrival
At the western edge of Birkenau

Glasses   shoes   luggage   jewelry
Anything separable from the victim
Who vowed during the journey
Never to surrender a thing

Call it the loss of one's identity
One's memory   one's hold on reality
Before that final and objective
Revelation of self as the last

Piece of hair falls to the ground
For transport to Germany   call it a cruelty
That deprives the spirit of the material
That denies the soul's dream of the body

By stealing each object of desire
What a telling story a worn shoe
What a sad arrival a piece of luggage
What a vanishing point a locket of hair

Selection

During "selection" at Auschwitz, prisoners unwittingly guided family members into groups designated to be gassed, thinking they would be saved.

How many times did a distant train
Whistle the approach of more families
Burdened by the weight of an idea
Visited upon them by the Third Reich

How many times from cramped train cars
Did they emerge to the shout of orders
And one tall figure in dress uniform giving
Direction with a leather stick to go right or left

How many disembarked in the morning gloom
As a single throng of people struggling
Not to lose sight of each other when guard dogs
Lunged forward and parted them like a school of fish

Whole families made to undress on the platform
Their belongings fashioning a small hill
The whole scene suddenly diverted from
Avenues of reason to questions without answers

Whole families faced with a moment's decision
Whether to keep the youngest with the oldest
Or encourage their separation   later to discover
The manifest heartbreak of love's good intentions

Little Wood

> *At Birkenau those selected for immediate gassing were brought to the Little Wood by Crematorium IV to wait and be photographed by the Nazi SS.*

How unholy under the darkroom safelight
As images of prisoners begin to appear
Ghost-like on photo paper   everyone
Gathered with family in the Little Wood

Huddled together against fear
Or the elements of the coming night
Desperation shows no other countenance
But faces edged with sharp expressions

And sidelong glances at the photographer
Who captured them settling among the trees
As each image deepens in perspective
One sees children ready to entertain

Stepping in front of their mothers to dance
For the camera   or for a closer look
How many finally emerge from the distance
Blurs with overexposure and the shapes of trees

Too much light summons the spectral
Too much shadow darkens the mind
Each image ruptures from one into the other
From cloud-white paper into ash

Clouds

> "Papa and I recognized Mama and Pola. They timidly covered their yellow Star of David patches and waved to us as we passed. We stared back, our hearts as heavy as the dark clouds above."
> —Benjamin Jacobs

Through the eyes of children at first
They glided slowly along the rafters
The full length of the barracks
White clouds with swirling centers

Some churned continually from within
Over the heads of sleeping prisoners
Newly arrived by train and gathered under
Painted slogans like "Work Makes You Free"

But then there were more   and watched closely
Several seemed to blow along the narrow roads
Between cell blocks and other buildings
Someone even mentioned their presence as far away

As the crematoria   like puffs of smoke
But not really smoke   colder   vapor-like
Collapsing into a center like the forming of a fist
Then expanding larger into view   all in one motion

Dark clouds the guards never noticed
When raising a hand to strike a woman or child
Or opening the door of the gas chamber
To untangle the dead who could only stare

Distant Music

> *Many of the camps had their own orchestras made up of inmates that would perform when new prisoners arrived, setting a "positive" tone.*

When the orchestra plays everyone knows
Another train spills forth its passengers at the ramp
They heard the same music the day they arrived
Sunlight like knives when the train doors opened

Strauss's Radetzky March conveys a light
Victorious strain that seems to collapse
Under the weight of the moment
Even the guards notice how subtly

The notes fall like everyone's hope during selection
But the orchestra plays each time
As though detached from the scene   or drifting
Across the flat surface of the ground

One might imagine a large hand
Holding the sound of the instruments
Or the musicians themselves sitting in its palm
Floating within their own distant music

That was everyone's memory
And each time the orchestra plays
Everyone knows they can only listen
To music the dead know best

The Bademeister

Cold water baths were a very cheap method for exterminating ill or exhausted prisoners

From where such ideas come is unknown
But bathing prisoners to death at the Gusen camp
Heinz Jentzsch saw as his final solution
A calibrated idea of death to surpass all reason

And so the "Bath-Attendant" steps forward
Not with towel on forearm or soap in hand
Not with the gentle tone of a servant's voice
Or a concerned look for his guests

But a smile at the efficiency of his method
Perfected in the dim hours of the morning
When small ideas seem large and the world
Collapses into the realm of a single filament bulb

One can see him   accompanied by his shadow
Testing the water for a paralytic chill
That would render the brain's image glacier-white
Lock the words of the screamer in his throat

Normally one might choose bath over hanging
And weakened by forced labor welcome the water
Were it not for the singularity of the idea
Whose persistence drips in the mind of the Bademeister

Clay Faces

> *Dvora Kurliandchik (Kantor) made clay heads while digging in the muddy canals at the Libisch-Graz Labor Camp. A German soldier gave her bread for busts of his family.*

How many faces arriving from the darkness of memory
Find their way into the gentle hands of a prisoner
Forced to dig canals in the mud and clay of the Libisch-Graz camp
How many faces take form under the sculptor's careful eye

While others around her melt under the glare of the commandant's
No doubt there were days when Dvora   like a medium
Conjured likenesses in shape and form
From the equally dark worlds of the living and the dead

How hopeful if one can imagine pressing the clay
Into familiar shapes   rounding the cheekbones   tapping the lips
Until a face appeared   risen from the earth
How odd they must have seemed   strangers even to her

Mud-pools in the twilight made windows through which others
Were pulled   even saved if one has that kind of faith
Perhaps the German soldier glimpsed into that world once
And thought of his own children held by loving hands

He brought Dvora fresh bread and pictures of his family
And from the clay of the earth she lifted them too
With their curious expressions   their dim smiles
A fear in their eyes for what their father would bring them

Roma

> At the Belzec camp in Poland over one hundred thousand gypsies, "Roma,"
> were murdered.

She stands alone in the snow   her boots without laces
What appears to be a coat sprawled on the ground beside her
Her hands clutched together under her chin
She pleads to whomever is behind the camera

An SS guard waits to her left and Ukraine collaborators
Stand in the background near some trees
If one looks closely her blouse fringed with lace
Laps her ankle-length skirt   a patchwork of designs

This photograph was found on a German soldier
She has no name   she is more alone than anyone in the world
Her bandanna clings to her head and her dark hair
Hangs loosely about her shoulders and reveals a single earring

I imagine several behind the camera   one giving orders
The others knowing only their "duty" on this winter day
She has no name   but I would say she's in her forties
And her life was always difficult   she had begged before

As a child perhaps for food   as a woman for compassion
Now she stands alone on this cold planet with no one
Surrounded only by the messengers of the Belzec operation
Call her Marie   lift up her eyes to the hills   keep her from all harm

Dr. Injection

> *At Gusen, a Mauthausen sub-camp, Dr. Eduard Krebsbach used heart injections as a method for executing inmates and preserving organs. He became known as Dr. Injection.*

Little wonder the heart's needle at Gusen meant death
Dr. Eduard Krebsbach's proclivity as surgeon
Favored the efficiency of that single procedure
For his ultimate intention   the harvesting of organs

Kept like rare items in bottles on the shelf
Some diminished through experimentation
Others procured through uncommon practice
The vestiges of prisoners whom he thought inferior

No need to ponder life while in the hands of the doctor
With his precise method for killing and his need
To fashion a victim's face into a death mask for his wall
No need to wonder about the destiny of one's head

It would be found   as paperweight on the doctor's desk
Or gift of the strangest order sent to a Berlin friend
Some examples of his medieval science
Finding their way to the SS Medical Academy at Graz

Where displayed as specimens of an inferior people
Displaced from their homes they added to Nazi intrigue
As though some purpose of mind had placed them there
For the benefit of all   a greater understanding of humanity

The Secret

> *"One by one in the dark, the ghosts who are our companions approach."*
> —*Primo Levi*

Who better than they remembers
Their last steps before collapsing in the sun
Awkwardly   skin-covered bones
And that stare death is famous for

Who better than they knows the impossible
One moment life   then life in death
And that final pose as though
Listening to wheels turning underground

Their hands were open   but empty
They held nothingness by the handful
And carried it with them until
Handed the eternal flames

Now with death's greatest secret
Barely comprehensible to the living
Like some vague understanding
Of something that happens so naturally

As not to be noticed by anyone
Rising   they approach from a distance
As we remember them following others
Through barbed fences into the visible world untouched

Her Face

> Besides his private experiments at the Gusen camp, Herbert Heim, the "butcher of Mauthausen" specialized in the preparation of human heads and faces for display.

Perhaps he examined thousands of faces
Some more beautiful than others
Some locked in final expressions of terror
Their lips holding the shape of last words

Yet this face he selected from the rest
As either the exact one
Or one embodying all others
On which a man's hatred might focus

A hatred in kind that transcends all proportion
That if held to the full measure of the heart
Would arrest the workings of the soul
This face hangs now on the wall

As would a picture   or a mirror
Whose reflection captures a primal stare
That overwhelms what were the familiar
Features of a human face   a woman's face

Once known as mother   daughter   or wife
Whose blush rose at the sound of her name
Grew radiant with the awareness of love when held
By other hands gentle enough always to comfort her

Planet Auschwitz

> *Survivor Yechiel De-Nur coined the name "Planet Auschwitz" while testifying at the trial of Adolf Eichmann. "I was there for about two years. The time there is not the same as it is here, on Earth. (…) And the inhabitants of this planet had no names."*

Some might recall Dante and his gates of hell
That point of crossover from the temporal to a grim eternity
Others might delve deeper to a point in space so dense
It's the absolute absence of everything   a black hole

A third calls out from sleep   from somewhere else
Marking the very center of the mind
Image-locked in a dimly lit room in cell block 10
An even darker place than imagined

The raspy breath of children frosting the window panes
The harsh winter cold clinging to the stone walls
They call out one minute to the next
Under the gloved hand and masked face

Of a doctor whose eyes float forward above them
In the naked light over the examination table
There are forms of cruelty that defy description
Recognized by the heart as coming from the other side

Outside one sees a body cart's burning wheel
Blackened by fire's consuming efficiency
Under a smoke-filled sky that defines a place
Unlike any other   whose name is farthest from earth

Angels

> *Imprisoned for protecting Jews, Dr. Adelaide Hautval of France, called "the saint," at Auschwitz refused to participate in medical experiments with Josef Mengele. Yad Vashem named her righteous among nations.*

The Angel of Death paces in Cell Block 10
The sound of his boots like clockwork
In the minds of those scheduled for surgery
The Angel in White appears somewhere else

As from a distant shadow
Come to hide them before selection
Hers is the gentle smile of hope
Barely visible by early light

Hers are the subtle methods of grace
That seem to alter reality
When moving them from a hallway bench
To isolated rooms for care

Upstairs   unseen in the high bunks
They will survive another day
And her memory of them conveniently fades
Perhaps they passed without her knowing

Perhaps she lost count of them that morning
She says   before retiring to her room
The afternoon light dimming to a milky haze
Even the Angel of Death grows weary by

Anne Frank

> *The Frank family hid for two years in the "Secret Annex" at Prinsengracht 263 before being betrayed and sent to concentration camps where all but the father died.*

What the astronomer tells us
About starlight   how light travels
Light years before appearing
In the corner of a sleepless night

Makes one want to remember her face
Dimming with the passage of time
Hers was the one overlooking
Amsterdam streets from an attic window

Annexed to an even colder world
She watched closely as passersby
Moved in their daily orbits from
Residence   to market   to post office

And what the astronomer says we see
Loses its source of light long before
Disappearing from view
And once gone there is an absence

Painted with the sheen of obsidian
Deepening the night with an emptiness
One feels when looking for a face
In a distant window

The Stairs of Death

> *At the Mauthausen camp prisoners were forced to climb the 186 steps of the Wiener Graben with large blocks of granite from the quarry on their backs until they succumbed under the strain.*

Each block of granite tied to a wooden rack
Is strapped to the man's back
Never mind the narrow steps of the Wiener Graben
That ascend into the morning mist

Never mind their number or how they
Are counted with each swollen foot
One hundred and eighty six moments
In a life that grows nearer the clouds

And if one were to drop the 50 pound stone
Cut by hand from the quarry wall
Would it fall to the ground
Stained by the blood of thousands

Or drift through the timeless ether
Guided by those who once held it
Only to arrive in the dreams of others
Their unexpected burden in life

Perhaps one can imagine something worse
Only a man carrying a granite block would know
Something that grows more ominous with each step
As he climbs the stairs of death

Mittweida

> *Labor-weakened prisoners were promised "Transport to Mittweida" for restful resettlement and recovery. Mittweida was an SS code word for mobile gas chamber.*

How promising the promise of life when made a dream
For those weakened by hard labor
How soon the dream expands to include
An ideal place   a place like Mittweida far away

Or so prisoners believed working at Ravensbrück
Mittweida   nestled in Saxony was the destination
The commandant promised when their condition demanded it
So the sick and exhausted boarded green panel wagons by twilight

For their journey along the narrow roads to Mittweida
Mittweida   its sound was green and lush   a meadow
Where the weak could bathe and under a full sun
Gather themselves into something they might recognize

Something from the past before the essential knowledge of self
Vanished from their faces for that stunned appearance
Brought by starvation and fatigue from digging ditches
Or pulling the stone wheel as punishment across the prison grounds

Yes   *Mittweida* was the answer   all agreed it was their dream
They would arrive there in the morning with their children
Among the shadows of trees peculiar in their lush detail
And all would find the accommodations surprisingly exact

Touched

> *Reinhard Heydrich, second in importance to Heinrich Himmler, was the leading planner of Hitler's Final Solution before being assassinated in Prague, May 1942.*

Photographed in black and white
The SS officer known by Nazis as the "Blond Beast"
Sits with a comfortable air and combed hair
Eyes fixed somewhere out of frame

His uniform is perfect for the occasion
Oak-leafed collar   SD arm patch and Socialist pin
Flying Eagle   even a Luftwaffe badge and Bars
For distinction in the service of the fatherland

What a surprise for him to look down
At the bloody mess of that uniform when attacked
Rounding a corner in Prague   the bomb stuffing it
Into his side before he staggered forth firing his Luger

What a surprise to have one's persona pounded
By the concussion of a blast ripping through the car door
Hitler called Heydrich "the man with the iron heart"
But death always has the last word

His photograph taken years earlier in an empty room
Shows the subject seated in an elegant wooden chair
His legs crossed   hands folded in his lap
The pose of a German officer beyond reproach   untouchable

Awake in Lebensborn

The Lebensborn project kidnapped thousands of "racially pure" children for indoctrination into the German master race. Some quietly resisted.

Himmler's project   his Aryan dream
He announced as the "Spring of Life"
And ordered Nazi patrols to spirit off
Blond-haired blue-eyed children at night

So the master race began one morning
With songs and promises of loyalty
Impossible for some to keep
Who still heard a different music

Taken from their homes they never
Surrendered family for so-called Nazi purity
They never warmed to the chill it brought
Rocked from the moorings of generations

They played along without forgetting
The nuances of their former lives with family
Those moments radiant as crystal
Catching glints of light from a distant place

While others embraced Himmler's project openly
And loved the booted swagger of their new father
They clung to their past as never too distant
To keep them awake in Lebensborn

The White Rose

Inspired by their father, Hans and Sophie Scholl along with Christoph Probst led the White Rose resistance group before being tried by the SS for treason. They were executed on February 22, 1943.

Perhaps their father's words of resistance
His passion   led them to imagine early
A new world only he could describe
Sounding in them a call to action

A desire for justice they would carry
As a commitment   as their special love
For a cause that went beyond words
Beyond what he had taught them

Perhaps his words struck a brassy truth
Amid their early years of silence
And in them finally rose up like one
Who pulls the bell rope with all his weight

Whose feet leave the ground momentarily
As the note tolls through the valley
A bright call of pure sound   for compassion
Diminished only by great distance

Perhaps they had always heard it
An intuited call for freedom
As in the White Rose resistance
Unmistakable in purpose

The Way Back

> *Separation of family members during the war was common–most times never seeing each other again, until joining them in death.*

On the other side everyone wrapped in light
Steps forward to greet you   saying their thoughts
Without voices   but with telling looks
Come to show you the way

So many now   stepping from the cloud
Dressed not in celestial gowns but clothes
As you remember them long ago in the ghetto
Before pushed into the streets for transport

Some faces are familiar   others are not
But all know from where you have come
Hair dusted with the ash of humankind
Scattered like a fog over the fields of Europe

Not one averts his eyes or ignores your thin hand
Reaching into the ether of their luminous void
Not one avoids touching your fatal wound
Now the very source of your longing

Of all the times pain has found its way into your life
And the dead seemed ready to welcome you
Who would imagine the perfection of light
As the way into their arms

The Portrait

> *On liberation day at the Flossenbürg camp, artist F. Van Horen insisted on sketching a portrait of his American liberator, Albert Salt.*

What joy leaps at the sight of a soldier
Come to save those who sit waiting at hell's gate
One might say the joy of thousands in the heart of one man
The joy of the living   and the dead he would never forget

Perhaps a joy so immense that sketching the boyish face of his rescuer
Was his only hope of containing it   keeping it whole
For passage back into humanity and home to Belgium
But how small humanity must have seemed after Flossenbürg

After long hours in the infirmary where a bed
Was a table-sized box one shared with a corpse
No doubt a man once   before diminished
Under the watchful eyes of the Lagerarzt

How small the world when the dead go unnoticed by everyone
But the artist   whose drawings capture the Nazi
Scheme to remove them from human history
One might think such compression of the spirit ends all faith

That the very image of a man vanishes
Under night and fog   unless saved by someone
Whose appearance carries the memory of joy
Whose own face is the very portrait of hope

Blondi

> *In the final moments in the Führerbunker, Hitler tested his poison on his favorite dog.*

What more could a dog do   than test her master's poison
With the Russians only a mile away
And the crackle of small arms in the distance
A walk in the Chancellery garden hardly seemed imminent

What can anyone do at the snap of leather stick on leather boot
But hunker down   tail lowered to defend one's flank
The doors were sealed and the plain concrete walls
Hardly masked the despair of the moment

Voices from the adjoining rooms   like muffled explosions
Echoed the final commands of an impatient master
Whose tight leash demanded obedience
And bold words barked of the fatherland

There were kinder days   when his dream of domination
Seemed to expand even a dog's world
When quiet moments defined a questioning face
Its expression drawn as on a wire between anger and bemusement

There were days while sitting on the ground next to him
The world seemed to parade by at attention
Of what else could a dog dream
Than something deathly to lay at her master's feet

Franziska Braun

Eva Braun's mother survived the war and her daughter by thirty-four years, dying in 1979 at the age of ninety-six. Her relationship with Hitler is unclear

What in the world is a mother to say
Her daughter some twenty years his junior   and him
Sporting that diminutive mustache like a black mark on his soul
He was one of any number of politicos from the bierhalle

But clearly his were the fiercest eyes of any   a wolf's
One might imagine a temper to match   a mean streak
Encouraged by Austrian nationalism
So what would a young Bavarian girl hope to gain by him

Amid the rock throwing of Kristallnacht and incessant rallies
That broke into riotous songs of the fatherland
A few collectibles perhaps   arriving mysteriously from Poland
Promises of a peaceful life together at Europe's helm

Perhaps there were days when a mother's doubts
Seemed misplaced   even short-sighted in the face of attention
He and others relished as they made plans for the Third Reich
Perhaps his rants made a sort of irrational sense

Through Eva's eyes when home for a visit   but no more
Some thirty years later a mother can only wonder at
The strange turning of events that seemed to wind their way
Through a time with her daughter too brief   yet all-consuming

White Rooms

> *At Dachau visitors stand in empty rooms that contain photographs from when they were filled with the corpses of victims.*

If time is the final measure of sorrow
Within these empty rooms at Dachau
Its apprehension spans years and is
Immense enough to account for thousands

Brought from the cities of Europe
To the site of their final moments
Together they entered this austere camp
Now whitewashed for history

Uncertain of their future or fate
And today we stand here without them
But feel their presence within
These white rooms and the

Cramped space of the gas chamber
The memory of thousands
Expanding these concrete walls unbearably
Crowding out rational thought with the irrational

With an inexplicable sense of self
Lost with them from a spacious world
Beyond words   beyond an awareness of time
Or the full measure of sorrow.

The Pond

> *The resting place for the ashes of thousands of people, mostly Jews, who were gassed at Birkenau in Crematorium IV.*

Under the surface of the water the shadows of hands
Move between sunlight and moon-glow
Dip and glide over subtle currents that shape   as in memory
The faces of the old and the young

Hands so numerous to count them would double anyone's grief
Hands so gentle in their touch that to walk into this pond
One might dream of being held by something other than water
Something construed from the past in darkness for all time

The hands of children holding the emptiness of the world
The hands of women waving goodbye from the train to Birkenau
One might dream of the shadows of hands in this water
As combs in the hair of the dead

This pond so far from life it captures no beauty in its reflection
Nor calms the soul borne from the body in silence
This pond like a slice of black ice in summer
An apotheosis of loneliness

Seems to exude the very breath of thousands
Their hands cupped over their mouths
In disbelief   in desperation of the moment
That deepens in us with each passing year

Blackbirds

Visitors to the Birkenau camp have noted seeing only blackbirds.

Winter at Birkenau hangs a solemn gray sky
Over snowy grounds spiked with dark fences
The gatehouse holds the search light
Called Black Flower for its bristled appearance

One might notice the silence were it not
For birds appearing suddenly overhead
Following them against a backdrop of gloom
They gesture like hands in black gloves

Directing prisoners from invisible train cars
That stand buffeted by wind at the ramp
Blackbirds are the only movement visible
And in their frenzied flight they mimic

Simple directives that swoop and dive
Along carefree lines of indifference
It is said that all the birds at Birkenau are black
And to watch them arrive on a winter morning

Is to see through time and be among those
Left standing in the cold   struggling
To understand   even imagine a fate
Tied to wings unable to lift a living soul

Spectacles

> *Upon liberation of Auschwitz, countless numbers of personal effects, such as eye glasses, shoes, and prostheses were found.*

Nothing tugs on the threads of reason
More than the number of spectacles found
Collected from prisoners at Auschwitz
Nothing dresses down what's impossible

As quickly as hard evidence
And given such variety and number
Who would expect denials of guilt by guards
Or some revised account of the truth

Look   a monocle tied with purple ribbon
Tangled among the many pairs of glasses
No doubt that of a Jewish aristocrat
Escorted with others from the ramp

How distorted the world would seem
Magnified through such a lens at night
How fluid those uniformed figures
Appearing from the darkness

Once taken   seeing would seem through water
Swirling in shades of green and blue
And breathing more difficult when engulfed
By their loud voices and barking dogs

Artifact

> *Excavations at camps like Belzec in recent years have unearthed
> numerous personal items from victims killed during the Shoah.*

Objects of interest are sometimes found
Unexpectedly   where no one would think to look
Suggesting a person's life in a different time and place
Presenting a point of focus for contemplating the possible

So one calls forth a scene where Max Munk
Pulls his silver cigarette case from his vest
And for a moment on a sunny Vienna morning
Watches the sunlight play across his inscribed name

Removing a cigarette he taps it lightly on the case
As sounds of Vienna are heard amid
Conversation and the light laughter of diners
The Cafe's name is unimportant but gathered there

Are the elite of the city for drinks and brunch
The waiters all meticulously dressed and serving
The day's catch on tables set with white linen and silver
Perhaps he joined them that morning   and later

Vanished under circumstances as cloudy
As the days would become before someone
Digging where the Belzec camp once stood
Found a cigarette case inscribed with *Max Munk of Vienna*

Whiteout

> *Prisoners with artificial limbs had them confiscated upon arrival at the camps. They were found piled in rooms at the camps.*

What kind of hope could one expect
Arriving at the Birkenau entrance on a winter's day
The blinding snow like a passage through time
What joy is even possible when one sees

The emptiness such a place holds   even now
An absence blurred by weather and time
Found at the edge of humanity
Its tower emerging from whiteout as one nears

Perhaps a need for something undeniable in the world
As simple as someone's life   imagined
Through some tangible object   like a wooden leg
Found among others collected at the ramp

Yes   the curvature of this limb calls forth a woman
Whose weight   whose identity   it held
Perhaps awkwardly at first   then hardly noticed
Until stepping forth under orders   or tested with a stick

This one sculpted in mahogany still wears
A shoe snugly on its foot painted red
Ready for its next step in the material world
Where all mortals must pass

Schindler's Grave

A memorial in the Park of Heroes in Israel praises Schindler as the Savior of more than 1,200 Jews. Yad Vashem named him righteous among nations.

Each stone lifted from the earth by a survivor
And carried in gratitude to the sarcophagus
Where Oskar Schindler's name lay carved under a summer sky
Each stone delivered there rests with others in his memory

As though drifting through space   time had placed them there
In odd formations along the perimeter and in small piles
For no other reason than unwinding destiny's sad ribbon
Over a parade of years to the very end in Israel

These stones of grief carried by each survivor
Who witnessed death at the hands of Goeth or Mengele
These collapsed stars whose density
And jagged shapes hold their memories

Now travel a still universe   years from the past
Locked in orbit around their enigmatic son
A man who stepped from the darkness alone
Fringed with the ashes to which all would succumb

Had he not been touched by an awareness
That settled with whispering voices around him
A reminder of a darker silence than death
To befall everyone but the righteous

The Blue Room

> *At Majdanek a blue byproduct of Zyklon B gas still lingers on the concrete walls of one of the gas chambers.*

Seen anywhere else one would say blue sky
Daubed with clouds illuminated by the sun
The blue seems that familiar   the various shades
Giving the walls a perspective of great distance

If one didn't know the truth
An imagined bird could easily fly away
And its song play so lightly on the ear
As to pass beyond a whisper

One might even walk there
Remembering such days when the world
Reached as far as one's love for it
When joy expanded it with each breath

But nothing is found here
Only concrete clouds and a blue residue
Cast at right angles to form this room
Never to be square with the world

Nothing of the remembered is left
But that imagined dark when the door swung shut
Latched   and final prayers
Filled a night as unfamiliar as the day

A.K.A. Ricardo Klement

Random statements from Adolf Eichmann's own defense at his trial in Israel following his arrest in Buenos Aires.

I am not the monster that I am made out to be
I had to switch from the unity of ethics to one of multiple morals
I am the victim of an error of judgment
And I would now ask the Jewish people on a personal level for forgiveness

I understand the demand for atonement
For the crimes which were perpetrated against the Jews
Acting on orders   I had to look at the atrocities
I am guilty of having been obedient

But I never...   I accuse the leaders of abusing my obedience
Obedience is commended as a virtue
My position is different   in this introspective examination
I have to ignore my sense of guiltlessness in the legal sense

Naturally I could not remember details with precision
I had to yield to the inversion of values which was prescribed by the State
I am not the monster that I am made out to be
Subordinates are now also victims   I am one of such victims

It was my misfortune to become entangled in these atrocities
The guilt for the mass murder is solely that of the political leaders
I had to engage in introspective examination in areas
Which concern my inner self alone   I was assaulted in Buenos Aires

for Rafi Eitan

Hairball

> *By 1972 Josef Mengele so feared capture his nervous habit of biting the ends of his mustache caused a hairball that blocked his intestines.*

Guilt wears many disguises   some recognized
Others hardly noticed like hair color
Or a mustache for hiding expressions
That might identify the patient in question

His demeanor was abrupt and impatient
As with the doctor who questioned his age
Curiously advanced for the forty-seven years
Claimed on his Argentine passport

And such an unexpected diagnosis for lower-track blockage
A hairball wound tight as an owl's pellet
Composed of excess mustache the nervous mouth trims
In expectation of a sudden knock at the door

How obsessed one becomes rolling each
Errant thought into one more threatening than the last
Each emerging from others   not as memories
But some hideous shape forming a genuine fear

Out of pieces of life and death at Auschwitz
Once reopened   the tangible compression of events
Spills forth the cruelties of that time
Arriving once again on dark wings

Woman in a Red Coat

> Dr. Martin Földi's account of his family's separation at Birkenau, and his daughter wearing a red coat when he last saw her, was first given at Adolf Eichmann's trial.

A photograph of the Birkenau train ramp
Shows a woman wearing a red ski jacket
Facing barracks to the north
Back to the camera   hiding her face from view

Perhaps her anonymity is fitting   it is winter 1996
And the grounds before her barren with snow
Perhaps she stands where a girl stood years before
In her red coat among strangers awaiting selection

That story   heard at the Eichmann trial
Left Prosecutor Gavriel Bach shaken   speechless
What it told is what one fears most   a child
Separated from parents   floating like a beacon

Through the crowd   passing from wave to wave
But the prosecutor was tied by a more ominous thread
His own daughter's recent present of a red coat
Now I study this photograph of a woman

Alone with her thoughts of the camp
And the cruelties intended to end all matters of love
The details of which assail the mind
Over what is impossible to escape

Questions

> *Many Nazis claimed no involvement in the Holocaust and, not being detained, returned to their homes at the end of the war.*

Questions of involvement received few answers
Lost in the smaller rooms of memory
Their involvement joined the realm of the forgotten
The unknown   suspended between

The unremembered and the unfathomable
How human failure so easily abandons the truth
Few understand   but consider how
Depraved their silence among the shadows

How they accepted a life of disillusionment
At the feet of a madman when false
Answers to each question seemed true
How they ignored their conscience

And dragging the flag of humanity behind them
They marched under a smoke-filled sky
Convinced of their own Nazi privilege
The blood on their hands no better

Than their promise of justice
With each passing day their indifference
For the lives of countless human beings
No more than a reason for ashes

Majdanek's Ghosts

> *At the Majdanek memorial the ashes of victims are displayed under a domed roof. Visitors claim to have seen ghosts there.*

None of them have the words to explain
Or the strength to lift their heads
But instead float forward motionless
Dusted in the ashes of years ago

Most drift nameless behind others known
If not by sight   through pictures
Or records   and seem caught
In a slow spiral toward the forgotten

No one says goodbye as more disappear
Because remembering is all that is left
No one waves   though many reach out
Their arms like ribbons on the wind

That so many of them gather around
Ashes domed like a volcano is no surprise
Ashes are what they have and voices
Like small vibrations in the damp air

None look back as they disappear
But the emptiness of space
Without them   with each departure
Expands our promise to remember

The Answer

> *"Those who cannot remember the past are condemned to repeat it."*
> *—George Santayana*

When the silence of six million souls
Assails the mind as nothing comprehensible
Like some awareness of space turned inside out
Its lifeless void appears an opaque cloud in the brain

And if one listens faithfully the silence is felt
As an absence of what no one can say
But larger than one's own life-sphere
That seems engulfed by it

An expanse that if illuminated by one candle
Would seem cavernous and into which
One might appear a conspicuous figure
Looking for the edge of light

For the limits of human grief
Contained by the silence of so many
But seeing the light's substance disperse
Merely dust the dark reaches

Ends all thought of deliverance
As one's sense of eternity comes sailing back
The presence of what might have been
The absence of a greater good

Gary Myers holds an MFA from the Iowa Writer's Workshop and a PhD from the University of Houston Creative Writing Program. While in school he studied under Donald Justice, Charles Wright, Marvin Bell, Jon Anderson, Stanley Plumly, William Mathews, Tom Lux, and Louise Glück. Upon graduation, he and his wife moved to St. Johns, Newfoundland, Canada, where he continued his writing career and taught creative writing at Memorial University of Newfoundland. After writing and publishing in Canada, Gary was recruited to the University of Houston as one of the first students admitted to the doctoral program in creative writing. His poems have appeared in the United States and Canada in such publications as *The New Yorker, Poetry, Kansas Quarterly, Louisville Review, Indiana Review, Crazyhorse, California Quarterly, Pleiades, The Albany Review, Poetry Northwest, The Plum Review, American Poetry Monthly, Descant, Bitterroot, Blue Light Red Light, Antigonish Review, Timbuktu, Poetry Toronto, Waves, Z Miscellaneous, Colorado-North Review*, and others. His chapbook, *World Effects*, selected by Naomi Shihab Nye as the winner of the Stanley Hanks Poetry Award, and sponsored by the St. Louis Poetry Center, was published by Nevertheless Press. His second chapbook, *Lifetime Possessions*, selected by Margaret Holley, won the 6th annual Riverstone Press Poetry Prize, sponsored by Bryn Mawr College. Myers is Professor Emeritus of English and Creative Writing at Mississippi State University where he served as co-founder of the Creative Writing program and later as Dean of the College of Arts & Sciences. He most recently served as Vice President for Academic Affairs and Dean of the Faculty at Young Harris College, Young Harris, Georgia. He and his wife Connie have raised a daughter, Jacqueline, and son, Timothy, and currently live in the mountains of north Georgia.

www.ingramcontent.com/pod-product-compliance
Lightning Source LLC
Chambersburg PA
CBHW030226170426
43194CB00007BA/875